PRAISE

"Jayne Martin's gift for conjuring moments of emotional betrayal is fearless, as is her keen eye for the everyday surreal. Dark, unflinching studies of fragility, identity, and the spirit's fight for survival, these masterful stories delight the reader with their generous, unconventional honesty."
MEG POKRASS, AUTHOR OF *ALLIGATORS AT THE GATE*, AND FOUNDING EDITOR OF *NEW FLASH FICTION REVIEW*

"Looking at the wounds and small triumphs of her characters from an often oblique angle, Jayne Martin examines moments in the lives of weirdoes and misfits, mutts and beauty queens. This is a collection that explores everyday drama, laying bare the tensions between anguish and resolution."
MICHELLE ELVY, AUTHOR OF *THE EVERRUMBLE* AND FOUNDING EDITOR OF *FLASH FRONTIER* LITERARY JOURNAL

"Here are stories that crackle with tough truths and meaningful reveals. It is remarkable with what agility Jayne Martin traverses such multi-various and rugged terrains. These pieces, though short, are expansive beyond all borders: bold, impactful, and thoroughly captivating."
ROBERT SCOTELLARO, AUTHOR OF *NOTHING IS EVER ONE THING* AND CO-EDITOR OF *NEW MICRO: EXCEPTIONALLY SHORT FICTIONS*

"Read the first line of any Jayne Martin story and I dare you not to keep going. A masterful storyteller, Martin's characters are funny, smart, wounded, and brave. These thirty-eight stories linger and satisfy. She does the work of a novel in a few pages with skill, grace, and power. A badass writer if ever there was one."
KATHY FISH, AUTHOR OF *WILD LIFE: COLLECTED WORKS FROM 2003-2018*

"Tender Cuts is about seeing and not seeing, what we are blind to and what's right in front of us. In this debut flash fiction collection Jayne Martin's writing is compact, dense, often heartbreaking, always illuminating, and woven with a strange nostalgia; she has a way of reconciling the child with the adult, the pain with the beauty of tragedy, the tragedy still seeded with hope."
NANCY STOHLMAN, AUTHOR OF *MADAM VELVET'S CABARET OF ODDITIES*, PROFESSOR OF CREATIVE WRITING UNIVERSITY OF COLORADO

"Jayne Martin traces lives punctured with regret, lost love, and dashed hopes. Surreal and real at the same time. A reader will leave these stories with a sense of healing, though, for Martin's storytelling knife is sharp with honesty and deft with insight into the vagaries of the human soul."
GRANT FAULKNER, EXECUTIVE DIRECTOR NATIONAL NOVEL WRITING MONTH; CO-FOUNDER OF THE LITERARY JOURNAL *100-WORD STORIES*

ABOUT THE AUTHOR

Jayne Martin's writing career began with a twenty-year stint writing movies-for television. Her credits include *Big Spender* for Animal Planet and *A Child Too Many*, *Cradle of Conspiracy* and *Deceived By Trust* for Lifetime. Her book of humor essays, *Suitable for Giving: A Collection of Wit with A Side of Wry*, was published in 2011. She has been the recipient of the following honors: Fall 2013 Women-On-Writing Flash Fiction Winner; 2016 New Millennium Writings Flash Fiction Finalist; 2016 Vestal Review VERA Award; 2017 Pushcart Nominee; 2018 Best Small Fictions Nominee. She currently lives near Santa Barbara, California where, when not writing, she rides horses and drinks copious amounts of fine wine, though not at the same time. Find her at *jaynemartin-writer.com*.

ABOUT THE ILLUSTRATORS

Janice Whitby has worked as a graphic designer for such companies as Disney and Hanna-Barbera designing packaging and logos, retouching photos and designing character illustration. She has also taught graphic design and illustration at various art schools in California. She can be contacted at janartist1@yahoo.com.

Indigo Roth is an writer, artist, photographer, and lover of anything daft or kind. He wrote and illustrated the surreal sci-fi fairytale TESTAMENT: FUNNY BADGERS for himself, and was delighted when other people liked it too. He lives with his beloved Lisa in the English countryside near Cambridge, surrounded by a cast of unlikely characters and a lot of empty pizza boxes.

TENDER Cuts

A COLLECTION OF VIGNETTES

JAYNE MARTIN

Vine Leaves Press
Melbourne, Vic, Australia

Tender Cuts
Copyright © 2019 Jayne Martin
All rights reserved.

Print Edition
ISBN: 978-1-925965-24-7
Published by Vine Leaves Press 2019
Melbourne, Victoria, Australia

No parts of this publication may be reproduced, stored in a retrieval system, or transmitted in any form or by any means, electronic, mechanical, photocopying, recording, or otherwise, without the prior written permission of the copyright owner.

This book is sold subject to the condition that it shall not, by way of trade or otherwise, be lent, resold, hired out, or otherwise circulated without the publisher's prior consent in any form of binding or cover other than that in which it is published and without a similar condition including this condition being imposed on the subsequent purchaser. Under no circumstances may any part of this book be photocopied for resale.

This is a work of fiction. Any similarity between the characters and situations within its pages and places or persons, living or dead, is unintentional and coincidental.

Cover design by Jessica Bell
Interior design by Amie McCracken

 A catalogue record for this book is available from the National Library of Australia

In loving memory of

Kathryn (Kathy) Hope Handley
from whom I first heard the term "flash fiction."
Thank you for taking me under your wing
and helping me find my tribe.

The beauty of the world has two edges, one of laughter, one of anguish, cutting the heart asunder

Virginia Woolf

TABLE OF CONTENTS

Tender Cuts ~ 13
When the Bough Breaks ~ 15
The Elephant Roars ~ 17
All Hallows' Eve ~ 19
The New Kid ~ 21
Zero Tolerance ~ 23
See No Evil ~ 25
Prom Night ~ 27
Twenty-Eight Days ~ 29
Blue Boy ~ 31
Making the Cut ~ 33
The Understudy ~ 35
Thanksgiving ~ 37
BFFs ~ 39
Morning Glory ~ 41
Cover of Darkness ~ 43
Dearly Departed ~ 45
First Impressions ~ 47
The Contract ~ 49
I Married a 1985 Buick LeSabre ~ 51
Night Shift at the Final Stop Café ~ 53
Carry Me Home ~ 55
Travels with Ivan ~ 57
Prime Cuts ~ 59

The Wedding Night ~ 61
Stepping Out ~ 63
Complicit ~ 65
This Is How You Leave Me ~ 67
Last Date ~ 69
Gone ~ 71
Working Girl ~ 73
A Lobster Walks Into a Laundromat ~ 75
In the Wake ~ 77
4Ever ~ 79
Eventide ~ 81
Birds of a Feather ~ 83
Pinky Swear ~ 85
Final Cut ~ 87
Acknowledgements ~ 89

Jayne Martin

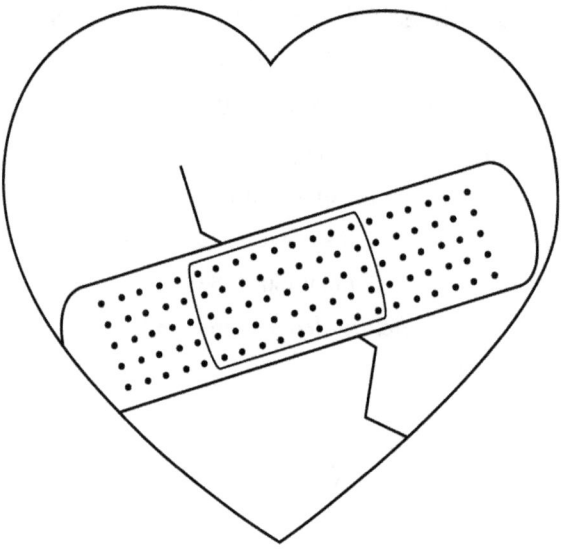

TENDER CUTS

Julie-Sue's hair cascades in golden ringlets past her tiny shoulders, falling near her tightly-corseted waist. The corset pinches her skin, but Mama says to keep smiling so she does. The "Little Miss Soybean Pageant" pays $150 to the winner and Mama says they need the money.

Next to the stage, the stench of livestock rises from a pen where the 4-H animals await their turn at auction. Flies swarm in the summer heat, and Julie-Sue bats them away from her face.

"Stop your fussing," Mama scolds.

She will dance the can-can just like she's been taught. She wanted to twirl a baton like Becky or sing a song like Bonnie-Jean. She doesn't like raising her skirt up and showing her panties, but Mama says she has nice legs and she should use what the good Lord gave her.

The auctioneer's voice rises and cheers explode from the nearby tent. Someone's prize heifer sells for a thousand dollars.

Her music starts and Mama pushes her onto the stage. She will kick as high as she can.

Jayne Martin

WHEN THE BOUGH BREAKS

If they don't get here soon, he is sure he will bust wide open. The bright yellow lily he'd picked for her this morning was already starting to wilt in the muggy heat of the Iowa noon.

Seems like it was just spring when his father had carried him up the ladder to a thicket of juniper branches where four tiny spotted eggs rested among the carefully-arranged twigs of a sparrow's nest.

"It's no bigger than that right now," his father explained.

He'd seen babies before, watched as his Aunt Ellen grew large and round as a pumpkin with his cousin, Ray. He knew they took a lot longer to hatch than sparrows. His mother, too, had grown large and round as a pumpkin. Some days she could barely get off the sofa. Her ankles had become thick purple rivers emptying into swollen ponds of flesh that he would rub as she stroked his head and called him her good boy.

"She's going to depend on you to protect her, you know," his mother had said.

He could do that. He was good at protecting things. When their barn cat tried to climb up to the sparrow nest, he'd chased it away with the hose and it never tried that again. He would hold her hand when they walked to the school bus, and teach her how to tell the good snakes from the bad ones, and when it thundered so loudly that their whole cabin shook and lightning lit up the sky for miles around, he would hide his own fear so that she would feel safe.

By then the baby sparrows had flown off, all but one that he had found lying stiff and cold at the base of the tree. When he had cried, his father said that was just nature's way sometimes, and together they had buried it and said a prayer.

He had clung to his mother's skirt while his father half-walked, half-carried her to their car. They told him not to worry about the blood that trailed from their doorway.

Soon dusk would begin to cast shadows like ghosts across their land. Still, he waited.

Jayne Martin

THE ELEPHANT ROARS

No one wanted to talk about the elephant in the room, except for the children who would talk of nothing else. We had adopted it when it was a baby, when we believed we could have no children of our own, when we believed our love for one another wasn't enough. The toddler snoozes in the curve of its trunk, while the twins cling to its sturdy legs, sucking their thumbs well into their teens. You lie on the sofa, clutching the remote, only your feet visible under the pachyderm's massive belly. I sit at my computer, chatting with wolves. The elephant roars, but nobody hears it.

Jayne Martin

ALL HALLOWS' EVE

It was the one day when she could roam the neighborhood streets just like any other child with no notice taken of the rags draping her tiny frame; her shoes, much too large, stiff and warped by rain, the laces long gone; her hair, once the color of the sun, now a dirt-encrusted mass of mats and tangles. Bright Eyes, she was called by the others who camped under the bridge at the edge of town, and indeed, her large green eyes shone like those of the cats who kept the river rats at bay. No one knew where she had come from for she did not speak, but she was one of them now and being a child afforded her no special privileges.

She blended in easily with the witches, goblins, and zombies who roamed the streets that night – beggars welcomed with a bounty of sweet treats – and eagerly scooped up the unwanted apples thoughtlessly discarded by children who had never felt the painful knots of an empty stomach. These she would devour on the spot, letting the golden juice run down her chin, leaving sticky tracks of sweetness in its wake.

Inside the houses were grownups eager to join in the night's fun: "Look at this little ragamuffin, honey," they would say, laughing as they tossed a candy bar – sometimes two – into her outstretched bag.

As the hour grew late, she watched the others return to their warm, clean homes where, costumes removed, they would once again transform into the children of privilege who would taunt her with words and stones should she dare to enter their world in the light of day.

But for this one night she was one of them.

Jayne Martin

THE NEW KID

Smaller than the other fifth-graders, a stutter to his speech, his clothes obvious hand-me-downs, he would arrive home from school each day bruised and bitter. Today, they'd strewn his bagged lunch across the playground. He had only intended to show them the gun.

Jayne Martin

ZERO TOLERANCE

Lights blaze from above day and night but give none of the sun's warmth. Around me the littlest ones grab onto the metal fence, cry out *"Mama," "Papa,"* and look up into the eyes of strangers in brown shirts who laugh at their terror. I will give the brown shirts no such satisfaction.

My eyes turn inward and I am back in the bedroom I share with my older brother, Ramon. My grandmother cooks huevos revueltos with carnitas for breakfast and sings the songs of our land learned at the knees of her grandmother. Mama calls for us to get up. We mustn't be late for school. Papa comes into the room. *You study hard today. Make your Mama and me proud, sí?* He kisses us both on our foreheads before going to the fields. His body is still not found by the time we must flee. Ramon, just thirteen but the man of the family now, gives himself up to del Cártel de Juárez near Chihuahua so that Mama and me may pass free.

At the border, they tell Mama they are taking me for a bath.

Jayne Martin

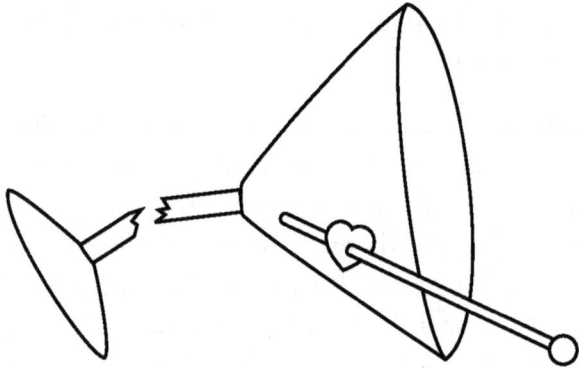

SEE NO EVIL

I sit on the floor in my pajamas, my nose only inches from the images flickering on the TV screen. My mother says this will ruin my eyes, but it is the sound that draws me close, holds me in its comforting embrace. It doesn't matter that the audience is not real, that what I hear is fake laughter. Only that it drowns out the angry voices of my parents, the crash of furniture when one stumbles and falls, the shattering of a thrown glass.

My mother needn't worry about my eyes. They are always closed.

Jayne Martin

PROM NIGHT

She descends the staircase in a swish of silver satin, uncertain on heels just a bit too high; her unruly curls now upswept from her shoulders, pinned and sprayed into place. She does not see his breath catch in his throat, the hand holding her corsage beginning to sweat.

He stands frozen in place like a serf at the feet of a queen, his starched white shirt sharp against the clean cut of his black tuxedo jacket, setting his spine straight and tall against his natural inclination to hunch. He does not see her heartbeat quicken or the slight quiver of her lower lip.

The glitter ball bathes the room in stardust and dreams as the dancers sway in each other's arms. Intoxicated by the scent of lilacs at the nape of her neck, her breasts full and soft against the thinness of his chest, he feels himself grow large with desire. He does not see her eyelids close or the images of ever after play out behind them.

Cramped in the back seat of his dad's Honda Civic, it is over sooner than either of them expect. They both hasten to cover tender flesh. She waits for words of love he does not say. He does not see the tears well in her eyes. He asks if it had been okay. She does not see him shove his hands under his thighs to keep them from shaking.

They pass in the school hallway. She, hidden under a mop of untamed curls. He, buried beneath the stoop of his shoulders. Bodies press in on them from all sides. Their arms brush. Their eyes meet for a heartbeat. They do not see.

Jayne Martin

JANUARY						
SUNDAY	MONDAY	TUESDAY	WEDNESDAY	THURSDAY	FRIDAY	SATURDAY
		~~1~~	~~2~~	~~3~~	~~4~~	~~5~~
~~6~~	~~7~~	~~8~~	~~9~~	~~10~~	~~11~~	~~12~~
~~13~~	~~14~~	~~15~~	~~16~~	♥	18	19
20	21	22	23	24	25	26
27	28	29	30	31		

TWENTY-EIGHT DAYS

She can't be pregnant because she only did it once and he wasn't even inside her that long and most of the stuff spilled down her leg anyway. "Do it. It's no big deal," Jessica had said, pouring the stolen vodka into the Sprite and pushing her into Bobby Morris, the cutest boy in class, who she couldn't even believe liked her. Kids were pairing off into other rooms, and the drink had made her head float like clouds that looked like angels, but weren't.

Her period had never been late before not that she'd had it all that long. Everyone else got theirs way before she did and she had faked cramps when her friends complained of their own, but now she could be pregnant and no way can she just walk into Walgreens and buy one of those tests because what if one of her parents' friends sees her. She lingers at the store's CD rack and then slips over to the aisle with the tests and how is she even supposed to know which one to get. She grabs the one with the cute baby on the front that kind of looks like Bobby and shoves it in her bag, but then thinks maybe she should buy something, so she gets the new Shawn Mendez CD, pays for it, and rushes out of the store feeling like she's going to barf because what if she had gotten caught and it's all so not fair.

Then she's locking her bathroom door and peeing on the stick and is it blue for yes and pink for no or the other way around and she thinks of the new Carter baby next door and how he smelled of fresh talcum and his sweet smile when she held him, but now she sees red drops of blood in the toilet bowl and then she's sobbing and she doesn't understand why she can't stop.

Jayne Martin

Happy Birthday

BLUE BOY

I was born three minutes before my brother, slid right out they said, while Kenny's struggle with the cord would nearly take his life before he'd drawn his first breath. Blue boy, they called him.

***

"Surprise!" They jump out from behind couches, chairs, and tables loaded with food. So much food. My chest constricts as if in the grip of a fist.

***

"Kelly. Wake up," Kenny shook my arm. It was still dark out.

At fourteen, Kenny had dyed his hair cobalt blue, and rarely left his room.

"Go away." I turned my back to him and burrowed beneath the covers.

"Happy Birthday," he whispered, and gave me a light kiss on my left cheek. Such a weirdo, I thought as I drifted back to sleep.

***

Someone takes my coat and bag. Someone else hands me a glass of wine. My trembling sends it shattering to the tile floor like a scream.

***

Pancakes in the shape of hearts bubbled on the stove. A birthday tradition.

"Go rouse your brother, Kelly," Mom said. Remembering Kenny's nocturnal visit, I burst into his room preparing to leap onto his bed and extract my revenge. His feet floated above floor, bare and already blue.

Friends brought food. So much food.

Jayne Martin

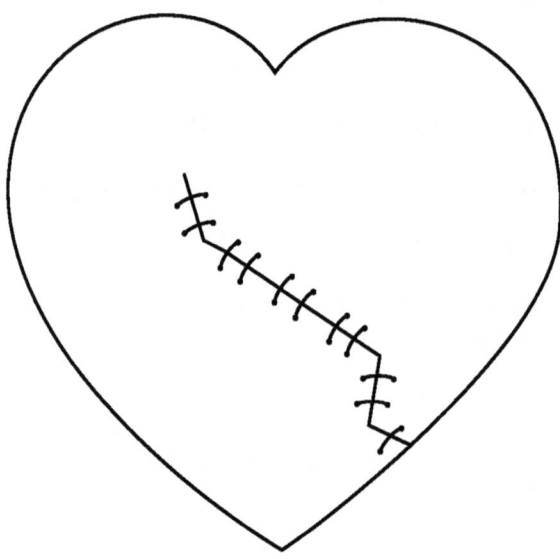

MAKING THE CUT

"Stop your squirming, Julie-Sue, or I'm gonna stick this pin right in your behind."

Her mother had saved her tips for months to buy the gold lamé fabric that now draped Julie-Sue's breasts and hips, buds that seemed to have sprouted into fully ripe fruit overnight.

"Let the others dress their daughters in frou-frou pink chiffon like damn poodles. You'll be the one catching the judge's eye, baby," said Mama.

"Mama, I'm tired."

"Oh, and you think I'm not. You think I enjoy standing on my feet six days a week washing those old biddies' hair to take care of us. Tired! Stand still!"

Julie-Sue knew better than to argue the point. She let her mind wander to the creek out back. How cool the mud felt squishing between her toes when she'd cross it to reach the Crandall farm on the other side. How she'd hide in the brush, her sketchpad in her lap, and draw pictures of Billy Crandall, his bare chest glowing with sweat, as he threw feed to the chickens.

"Okay, now turn around," Mama said, finishing the last stitch in the hem. She smiled, lit up a Salem from a nearby pack and blew a smoke ring into the air that hovered above Julie-Sue's head like a crown.

Jayne Martin

THE UNDERSTUDY

The single satin ballet slipper tumbles down, down, down the side of the building, landing on the city sidewalk below with barely a sound. There, among throngs of foot travelers oblivious to all but their digital devices, it is kicked aside several times before coming to rest at the soiled base of a traffic signal alight in red.

From her precarious perch at the edge of the roof high above, the wind slicing through the thin, damp fabric clinging to each step of her spine, Carmen watches the rehearsal continue in the building across the street, just three stories below. Slowly, she unties the ribbons of the other slipper and wonders what it will take for them to finally take notice of her.

Jayne Martin

THANKSGIVING

More vegetables, dear? You don't really need another biscuit. Easy on the gravy, darling. Pie anyone? No whip cream, honey. I nibble at my allotted portions that are nowhere near sufficient. It's true. I am large, yet Mother is peerless at reducing me to nothing at all.

Jayne Martin

BFFS

We snuggle deep into your bed pillows, banish your husband from the room because this is our time. You take off your wig, hang it over the bed lamp, your head a road map of scars, bald from chemo. It is the first time you've let me see it and I tell you that you are still the prettiest girl in high school. Then, because you would expect no less from me, I ask if I can sign it. You laugh and call me a bitch. You fill the high-tech blue plastic inhaler with medicinal-quality weed. No sticks or stems, no fumbling with ZigZags rolling paper like when we were young and sucking back on sloppy doobies. We inhale the sweet smoke, hold it in our lungs, and journey backward to the time of skin-tight skirts and dances at the "Y," first dates, first cars, first marriages. We laugh till we cry, and then we just cry.

Jayne Martin

MORNING GLORY

They cut you from my body as you rage against your removal. You'd grown large, claiming every ounce of me as your own like the morning glory that creeps over our mulberry bushes, strangles the sycamore and the spruce, swallowing everything in its path. Each summer, I hack and hack away at it, but I am no match for its appetite.

You attach to my breasts, suckling with fury, while I become emaciated in my struggle to provide. When I cannot, you turn your face from the offered bottle, burn bright with wrath.

The vines crawl beneath the doorway, steal through cracks in the walls, descend from the chimney. You will not sleep but in my arms, and I must keep moving lest they attach to my ankles and pull me under. My body sags under a cloak of exhaustion.

Inside the garage, I buckle you securely into your car seat. You scream in protest, but I have not the skills to soothe you. Already the morning glory seeks us out, slithering under the garage door. I rush to stuff blankets in its path.

I collapse into the driver's seat, roll down the windows, and turn the engine key. Its quiet purr calms you. I've finally done something right. We breathe in that which is invisible. The vines unfurl and slowly release their grip.

Jayne Martin

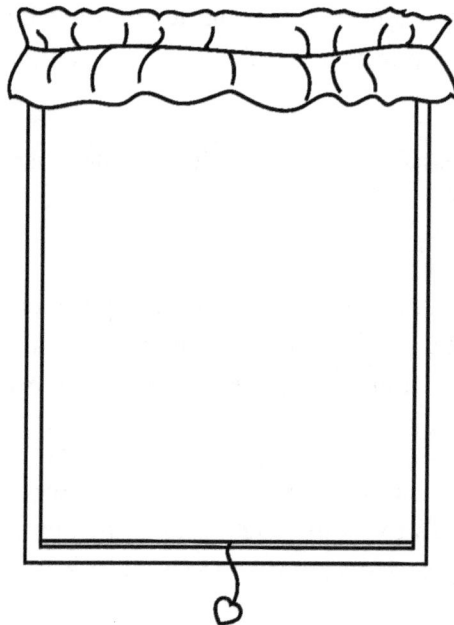

COVER OF DARKNESS

Anna quietly slipped out while he was still sleeping. He'd seemed a nice enough guy. Sam? Steve? Saul? She knew it started with an "S." A pink glow spilled over the edge of the Atlantic. Brisk salt air filled her lungs and she savored the taste of the new morning.

The brick steps chilled her spine as she sat to pull on her boots. She pushed the crisp bills down deep to her ankles where the money would be safe. She wasn't the only one who walked these streets at this hour.

At home, her babies would still be snuggled deep in slumber and smelling of cotton candy dreams. They would sigh at the touch of her lips and the warm curvature of her body as she slid beneath the covers, encircling their bodies with her own on the pull-out bed they all shared.

Anna's mother would rise first, set the kettle to boil. She would find the stack of bills Anna had left on the kitchen counter. And though no one could see into their fifth floor walk-up window, she would pull down the shade.

Jayne Martin

DEARLY DEPARTED

The overpowering scent of orange blossoms, although there wasn't an orange tree within miles of my Brooklyn brownstone, could only mean one thing. Mother was here. Raised amidst the orange groves of Florida, she had surrounded herself with its bouquet in everything from soap to candles to body lotion throughout her lifetime and she hadn't abandoned it in death either.

The tea kettle began to whistle, despite there being no flame beneath it. Oh, God. She wasn't just passing through this time. Mother wanted to talk.

Her visits had been pleasant in the beginning, just a whiff of orange now and then—a comforting reassurance that our loved ones lived on and still watched over us. But of course Mother couldn't just leave it at that.

"Hi, Mom."

I'd told none of the family about her visits, but for my birthday this year my older brother, Eric, had inexplicably given me a Ouija board, while taking pains to avoid eye contact. He'd always tried to push her care off on me.

The small, wooden heart sailed across the board under the light touch of my fingertips. Say what you will about my mother. She's nothing if not consistent.

"Yes, I have put on a few pounds ... No, Mother. That's not the reason I'm still single ..."

Jayne Martin

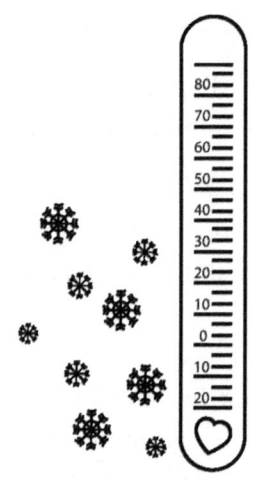

FIRST IMPRESSIONS

I had worn the wrong shoes, although they hadn't been wrong when I chose them. It's not like anyone had planned on this snow. Well, okay, some had planned. Some had even forecasted it. But how often were those people right? Besides, the shoes had been meticulously chosen to go with the strappy, festive dress. The dress that, as it turned out, hadn't been a good idea either. William had said his family were simple people but had neglected to mention the Amish part.

I shiver by the fireplace. Their dog licks my bare ankle, sticks his nose in my crotch while several children dressed as Laura Ingalls regard me as one might a two-headed goat.

I overhear his mother say, "Sweet girl, but none too bright, is she?"

His father brings me a shawl.

Jayne Martin

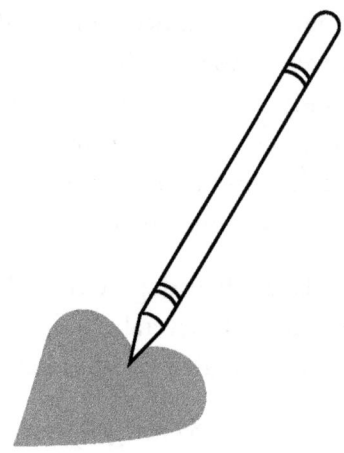

THE CONTRACT

He wrote it out on a cocktail napkin. He said it was still binding, even if he'd written it on a banana peel, as long as we both signed it. The bartender was a witness. I promised him complete fidelity while he was deployed. He promised me he would return. We both lied.

Jayne Martin

I MARRIED A 1985 BUICK LESABRE

He was solid, dependable, and had a spine of steel. Never a small woman, I felt dainty when I sunk into his embrace, his ride snug and gentle. He'd been married once before, and there were scrapes and a few dents to show for it, but under the hood his engine still hummed and I believed my heart could heal his.

"You're my reason for living," he'd say and for a long time that's how it was. We weathered the rough roads and gave thanks for our blessings over the smooth ones, him never once failing to get us safely home.

I suppose there were signs when it all began to change, things I didn't or chose not to notice. Always a morning person, he became slow to get started. The cough that he said was nothing until his whole body shuddered; the purr that became an angry growl of frustration. We were told that connectors in his brain weren't sparking like they used to, and some other parts needed work, too. But my husband was a stubborn man.

One day I awoke and he was simply gone. There was instead someone I didn't recognize: small and mean, roaring around the streets until all hours in the flashy colors of someone half his age. I tried to fit in with these new expectations, but there was simply no room for me. When I began finding parking tickets from neighborhoods a good distance from our own, he didn't even try to make up a story.

Police said they found him wrapped around a utility pole.

A long, black Cadillac now awaits me at the curb.

Jayne Martin

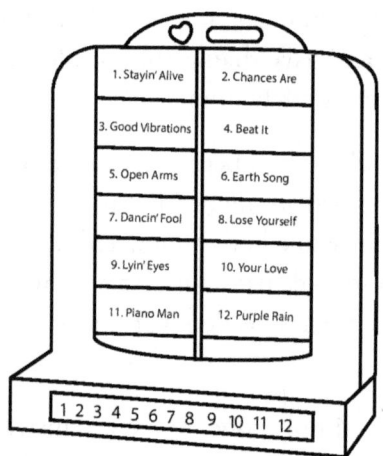

NIGHT SHIFT AT THE FINAL STOP CAFÉ

Quarter of four and he orders the last piece of coconut cream pie. Not the freshest I say, but he says he don't mind. He drops a dime into the tabletop juke. Johnny Mathis croons "Chances Are." He asks me to dance. My swollen, bare feet follow his out the door into the dawn.

Jayne Martin

CARRY ME HOME

He carried me when I could no longer carry myself. Barely able to stand on his skeletal frame when Dusty first hauled him home, the old paint gelding was now fat and shiny from spring grass and grain.

Dusty, always to the rescue. I'd never made my way out of the bottle if it wasn't for him. God knows before him, I had no reason.

"We'll call him Lucky," Dusty said.

"Damn right," I replied. And we both laughed.

There were days when he'd climb on Lucky with nothing but a rope draped around the horse's neck and they'd be off in the hills for hours. I never asked where they went or what thoughts he shared with that old horse that he didn't share with me.

On nights when Dusty would cry out, shake and soak the bed sheets with sweat and tears, I'd cradle him like a child, stroke the scar that stretched across his abdomen where enemy fire had ripped straight through.

We'd fought the night before they found his truck overturned in the flood basin. Who knows why he thought he could cross there. The early rains had left near thirty inches in three days and there was no letup in sight. No one right in the mind was out on those roads. That's what I'd told him, too, but downstream the Carter home was being washed away and Dusty had served in Iraq with their father.

Lucky nuzzles my pockets for carrots as I toss the rope around his neck. Around my own, a leather pouch holds Dusty near the cavity that once held my heart. I climb onto the old gelding's back and let him lead the way into the hills.

The thing is I already knew he was dead before the sheriff showed up at our door. I'd seen him at the end of our bed before dawn, young, smiling, and standing tall in his dress uniform. He held out his arms and I went into his embrace.

"You feel so thin," I said. And then he was gone.

Jayne Martin

TRAVELS WITH IVAN

As Margot tossed him off the icy Austrian peak, she marveled at how he twirled in the updraft and blew him a kiss as he disappeared from sight.

Ivan was a large man, half-again as wide as he was tall, while Margot was petite, the top of her head barely brushing against his nipple. Placing one of his outsized hands gently under her bottom, he loved to lift her up and call her his "Thumbelina," as if it were she who was of unusual mass and not he. Together they had traveled the world making memories at every destination, and she had promised to return him to the places he had loved most.

In his arms, she had felt safe, protected by the mighty fortress of his chest. Now she carried him around in Baggies.

Jayne Martin

PRIME CUTS

Julie-Sue squints into the damning July sun. The "Miss Teenage Soybean" sash rests across her ample cleavage where the Mayor's hand had lingered in its placement. That same hand now squeezes her behind as they stand side-by-side in front of a local news photographer.

"Smile, Julie-Sue!" her mother calls.

Later, sinking into the cool grass under a tall Sycamore behind the 4-H tent, Julie-Sue rids herself of the crippling high heels and tosses the tiara to the ground. From between her breasts she pulls a cigarette and matchbook and lights up, inhaling the Salem menthol deep into her lungs. Nearby, a family with a girl near her own age smiles for a photo next to the girl's prize calf.

The cheap plastic crown crumbles beneath the force of Julie-Sue's bare heel.

Jayne Martin

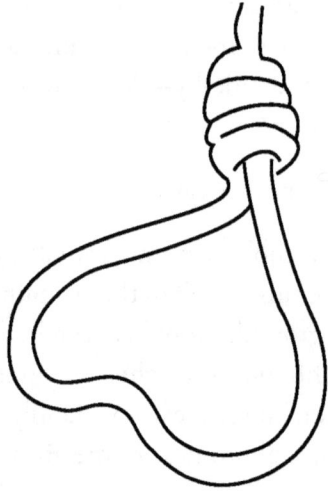

THE WEDDING NIGHT

Her knee slammed into the corner of the glass-covered night table as she struggled to sit up, the sharp pain serving to awaken her senses.

Outside, fog horns called to each other through a dense mist like giant beasts in search of their mate, while inside her bare foot brushed against the empty bottle of "Jose Cuervo" that had transported her from her own.

Her eyes began to focus, taking in the unfamiliar surroundings, until her gaze fell upon the discarded heap of satin and white lace lying on the floor, causing a swell of panic to encase her in its grip once again: The pounding of the church organ, the suffocating scent of a thousand gardenias, the eyes—so many eyes—bearing down upon her every step.

From behind, she felt him stir and his arm slowly encircle her—like a noose.

Jayne Martin

STEPPING OUT

The coat rack that once held the jackets, hats, and mufflers of her children now danced her across the room to the salsa beat of her Argentine roots. Her husband had been the last to go and still did not understand why he had gotten booted from the family home. The children, now with children of their own, called daily begging her to visit, but in such invitations she saw dirty diapers and meal-making, duties she had fulfilled and did not wish to revisit. While a bit stiff, the coat rack asked for nothing in return for its companionship, never once interrupting her tales of the more attractive suitors who had ignited her girlhood passions, or expecting dinner on the table at any prescribed hour. It did not leave cigar ashes on the rug, laundry on the floor, or demand its rights to her flesh. In its arms, she was the fiery Latina of her youth, hips gyrating, her long, thick hair tossed back, the center of attention in every dance hall that still lived brightly in her memory. In the quiet evening hours, they shared stories of tiny, snow-covered coats and how quickly they had been outgrown and knitted gloves that had lost their mates. And she bought the coat rack a fine, long wool coat with a crimson scarf like the one her father had worn when he had given her in marriage to the suitor of his choice believing with all his heart that it was for her best.

Jayne Martin

COMPLICIT

At the mailboxes, I share sidelong glances with the neighbors from 3C and 4A as he arrives home. "Evening, ladies," he says, the stench of drink in his wake as he staggers up the stairs.

In bed, I pull the quilt over my head to shut out his rage. Turn up the television when your body slams against the thin wall we share. Avert my eyes from your bruised flesh when we meet on the landing.

The newspapers say we were complicit. I can still hear your cries.

Jayne Martin

THIS IS HOW YOU LEAVE ME

I blow out the match; lay its seared tip against the soft flesh of my inner arm, raising another tiny red welt. A shroud of fog, wet and dense, devours me. Headlights from another car that is not yours round the corner. I draw the cigarette smoke deep into my lungs to stave off the scream of your name.

Moths hurl their bodies against the lone street lamp that now bears all my weight. Through the darkened window of the closed café, I see us. We sit at a corner table, share a bottle of Chianti. Your fingers curl around mine, lift them to your lips.

My phone vibrates with your final words.

Jayne Martin

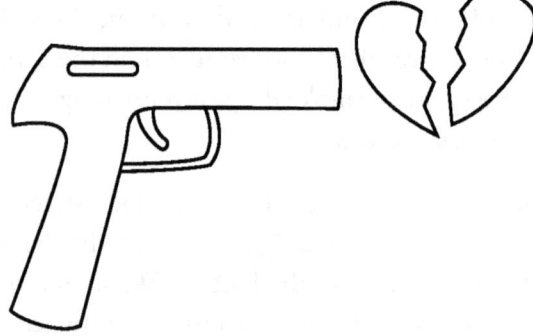

LAST DATE

The second hand ticks off another moment of my life. Waiting couples eye my table. I pretend to sip from the empty cup, lick the last bit of foam.

You arrive from her bed flushed, rushed and unapologetic, wearing the sea-green cashmere V-neck I gave you for Christmas. My finger tightens around the cold, smooth steel nestled in my lap. A real shame about that sweater.

Nobody wants my table anymore.

Jayne Martin

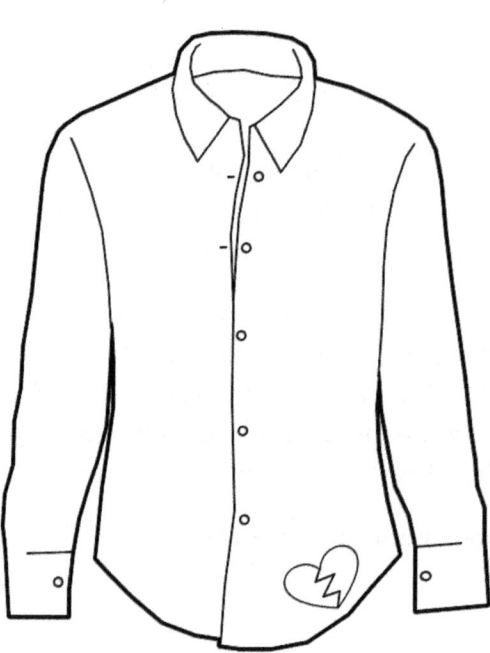

GONE

The shirt was neatly pressed just the way he liked. She'd hung it on the refrigerator door where he'd be sure to see it first thing as he entered through the garage. He'd wonder where her car was at that hour and why the house was so quiet. He'd call out for Buddy, his beloved schnauzer, who was usually leaping against the kitchen door barking to greet him. At first he wouldn't understand, but the large burn mark on the shirt hem would draw him close and the trace of red still visible underneath would bring his memory into sharp focus.

She'd laid the hot iron against the lipstick stain again and again as she thought about the woman who'd put it there. She knew her well. She'd been her at one time before the years had made her, too, replaceable.

The sea breeze washed over her, taking the past with it as she sped up the coast. She imagined her husband picking up Buddy's empty food dish from the floor; maybe going to fill it before he remembered just how alone he was now.

Her cell phone rang. She looked down at the screen. From the back seat, Buddy barked as he tried, over and over, to catch the wind in his mouth. She smiled and tossed him the phone.

"It's for you."

Jayne Martin

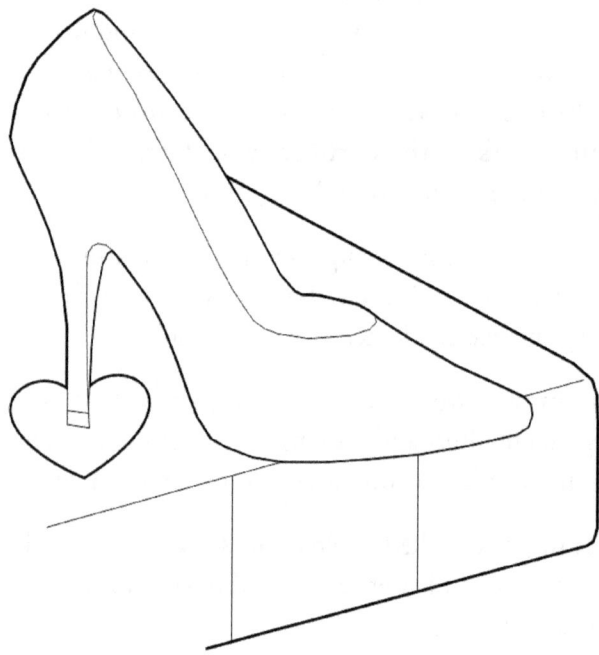

WORKING GIRL

Found upright at the curb in the chill of dawn, the single blush-tinted stiletto was the last footprint she would leave on this earth, its mate too quick to step into the car of another faceless stranger. Tiny hands press against a window and wait for her return.

Jayne Martin

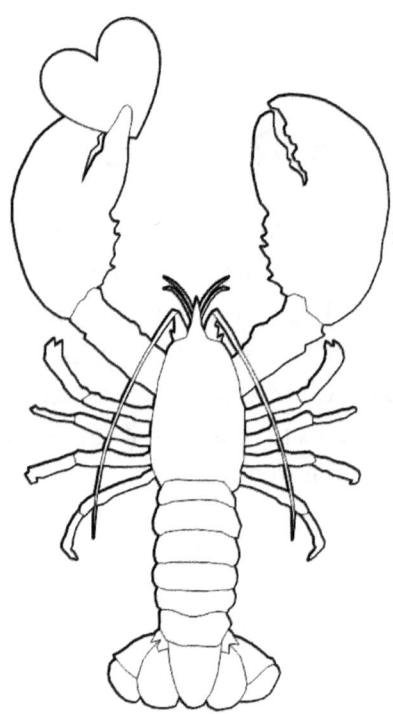

A LOBSTER WALKS INTO A LAUNDROMAT

None of the women could recall when the lobster first appeared, his large claws clacking against the floor as he folded his laundry along with the rest of them. He would arrive on Mondays, nine a.m. sharp, dragging a small cart brimming over with mostly napkins and tablecloths, and smelling of butter. While not much of a talker, every so often a sound like that of a bow across the strings of a violin would emit from him and though the women weren't clear about its meaning, they were charmed nonetheless. On occasion, one of them would swear that he'd winked at her and blush at the flutter it aroused.

It had been years since any of them had been noticed in "that way" and they had grown complacent about cosmetics, drab about dress, haggard about hair-dos. But on Mondays, lipsticks with names like Crimson Crush, Potent Peach, and Orange-U-Hot would shine from newly-painted lips and the scent of Aqua Net would hang in the air.

Between wash and rinse cycles, the women would vie for the lobster's attention with tips about stain removers and fabric softeners, and the lobster would listen, attentive as if they were spouting sonnets or Shakespeare and each woman would feel special and seen.

And they would return to their homes and husbands, lusty with demands the husbands would not understand but would nevertheless acquiesce to until about Thursday, when the monotony of their days would cause the women to forget themselves once again.

Jayne Martin

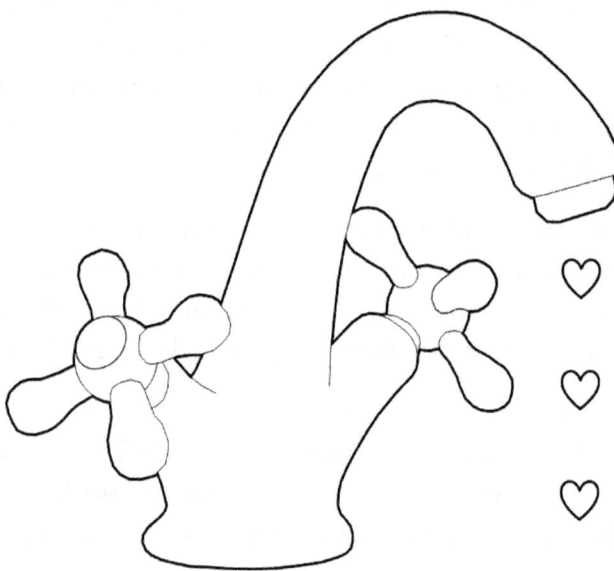

IN THE WAKE

The kitchen faucet he'd kept saying he'd "get to" continued its *plunk, plunk, plunk* into the aluminum sink. His idea. I'd wanted porcelain.

"Aluminum is cheaper," he'd said.

I'd threatened to call a plumber at fifty-five dollars an hour.

"It doesn't need more than a sixty-cent washer. I'll get to it."

I knew that. I could have fixed it myself any day I wanted to. I don't know why I didn't except I think I just wanted him to do something for me. It seemed like a lifetime since he'd pressed his naked body against mine, flooding my insides with his heat, clinging to me like a life raft in a thunder storm.

The refrigerator was packed with well-meaning casseroles, as if I could eat my way out of sorrow. Ice clamored into my glass. I poured another shot of Stoli. The *plunk, plunk, plunk* like the rhythm of a heartbeat now.

I'll get to it.

Jayne Martin

4EVER

As the wrecking ball closed in on the old stone structure, those of us left who still bore memories gathered in the parking lot and sang the school anthem. Few of us could argue that it was time. Transients and bored teens had been breaking into the place for years.

Somewhere in the pile of discarded desks was one with "JM + GR 4ever" carved on its blond wood face. I'd used the pointed end of the heart-shaped pendant you'd given me for my sixteenth birthday. Two years later, I'd enter Ohio State and you'd ship off to someplace called Vietnam that none of us had ever heard of. The boy who returned was as hollowed out as these ancient hallways. Still, it's good to see you here today.

My husband's arm slips around my waist. I lean into his side, grateful for the good life we've been given, while my hand finds its way to the delicate gold chain encircling my neck even now. I wonder if you ever think of me.

Jayne Martin

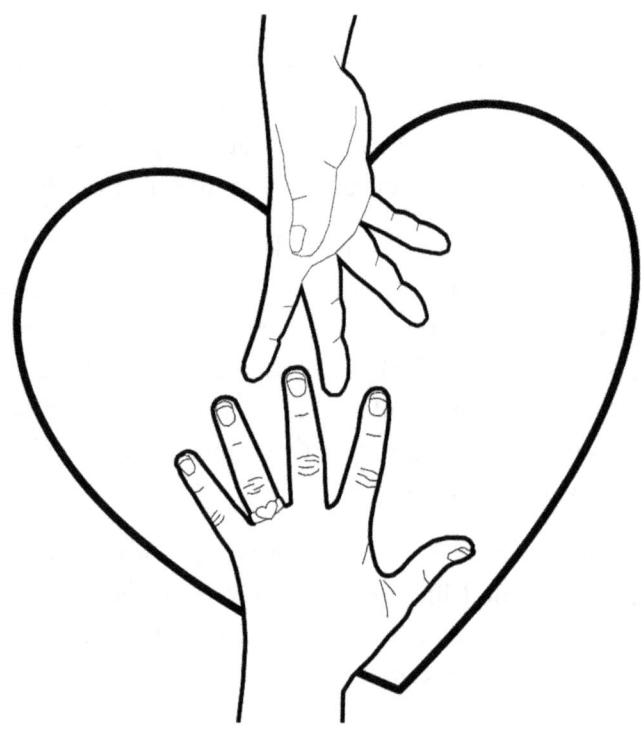

EVENTIDE

Your face is the first to fade from memory; still your voice, a bow caressing the strings of a cello, holds me close. Your scent, evergreens dipping to the sea shore, calms me on days when I cannot locate your name. I am running in the woods that stretch across the hilltop behind our homes—skinny legs and brand new Keds, my ponytail sailing behind. Leaves crunch beneath my feet as woodland birds take flight in our path. Fingers of sunlight reach through branches heavy with pine cones that will one day decorate a mantel hung with stockings bearing chocolate, nuts and oranges, children's names we will choose together, names that now reside only with you. I laugh and run ahead fast enough for you to give chase, but slow enough that you will always catch me. And you always have, caught me, taken my hand in yours and guided me home. But now I drift to where you cannot follow, where I am lost to even myself and the sun must bow to the rising moon. A nightingale sings at my window. At my bedside, the photo of a young couple in wedding attire, beautiful strangers. I had a beau who looked just like you once. Dance with me, you say.

Jayne Martin

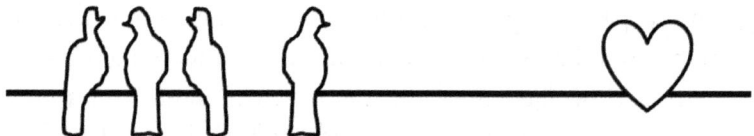

BIRDS OF A FEATHER

They gather at the same time and place every Friday, sitting side-by-side on the old, wooden bench like a flock of finches upon a wire.

Bundled against the cold morning air, these five men—friends since they had played stick ball in this same park as youths—sip from thermoses of hot coffee and munch on fresh-from-the-oven bagels from Happerstein's Bakery just across the street. Pigeons as gray as the stubble protruding from their chins gather at their feet for handouts.

In unison, the men's attention turns to the path on their left from which the women will soon appear. "Morning doves," they call them. It matters not that heavy sweatpants and parkas have replaced the revealing shorts and tank tops of summer. It is the women's smiles—sometimes a wink, often a little wave—as they jog past that the men wait for.

Jayne Martin

PINKY SWEAR

The caustic odor of rubbing alcohol burns my nostrils, settles on my tongue. A nurse paints Vaseline on my parched lips. I can't remember the last time I was kissed. I am tethered to tubes, encased in a coffin of withered flesh and bone that ignore all commands.

The growing cries of gulls, boardwalk barkers, laughter and shrieks of excitement begin to flood the room.

I sit in the car of a rollercoaster as it chugs and bumps up the steep incline toward the point of no return. Braver kids raise their arms high over their heads. I squeeze my eyes shut until it's over, say, "I want to go again," and am relieved when you do not.

We stroll the sandy walkway where we smoke cigarettes stolen from my mother's purse and flirt with boys. We make up names, Bridgette and Marilyn. Names that sound older and sophisticated unlike our own. We fool no one.

A pipe organ bellows. With fingers still sticky from cotton candy, we board gaily-painted steeds, ride round and round seeking the brass ring, stretching as far as we dare.

Our bodies distort in fun house mirrors and we wonder who we will become.

Pinky-swear friends forever.

The nurse rolls my body over to slip a fresh sheet beneath, and I see you by my bedside. You wear our favorite sweater, the rose one we passed back and forth until it unraveled, your smile still a mouthful of braces, your hand outstretched to me. In it, a shiny brass ring.

Jayne Martin

FINAL CUT

The odor of charred wood hangs in the air as I pick through the remains of the old garage. Most of the stuff had been Julie-Sue's. Rusted-out cans that had once held paintbrushes and tubes of bright acrylic promise; stacks of canvases unfinished or unfilled, all of it now ash. Mama had fancied herself an artist, a sculptor, anything but a former beauty pageant queen with a gaggle of kids.

"I can't breathe," she'd say and then walk off into the woods behind our house, disappearing for hours.

"Your mama's just a little bit sad today," Daddy would tell us.

Other times we'd come home from school to find her dressed in her fanciest taffeta, hips swishing beneath the stiff fabric, hair a mass of wild blonde curls, and The Rolling Stones blasting from the record player. How she loved the Stones. We'd all join in and Mama would be in a real good mood for a time. But then she'd take to her bed again, her weeping forming a pool of sorrow at our feet.

Glass crushes beneath my boot. Sticking up out of the rubble is a singed picture frame. In it, a drawing she had done: A self-portrait, crows tearing at her bare breasts. I recall seeing it as a child and how it had frightened me. My thumb catches on a splinter of glass and the frame falls from my hand. I taste the blood of my mother.

From our porch, my daughter calls to me, but the call of the woods is strong.

ACKNOWLEDGEMENTS

My eternal gratitude to the friends, mentors, and teachers who have guided, supported, and encouraged me on this journey. To name them all would be a book in itself, but they know who they are and how dearly I hold them in my heart.

To the journal editors who gave these stories their first chance at an audience, you rock my world: "Tender Cuts," 2018 Best Small Fictions nominee, *Moonpark Review*; "When the Bough Breaks," *Midwestern Gothic*, *Vestal Review* 2016 VERA Award; "A Lobster Walks Into a Laundromat," *New Flash Fiction Review*; "See No Evil," *Literary Orphans*; "The Understudy," *Spelk Fiction*; "Working Girl," *Blink-Ink*; "The Elephant Roars," *formercactus*; "Blue Boy," *Blue Fifth Review*; "Prom Night," *Crack the Spine*; "Morning Glory," *Five:2:One*; "Cover of Darkness," *Cabinet of Heed*; "Dearly Departed," *Spelk Fiction*; "Nightshift at the Final Stop Café," *Blink-Ink*; "Carry Me Home," *r.k.v.r.y*; "Travels with Ivan," *Literary Orphans*; "The Wedding Night," *100-Word Story*; "Complicit," *Drabble*; "Last Date," *National Flash Fiction Day, NZ-2016*; "Gone," *Boston Literary Magazine*; "In the Wake," *Dime Show Review*; "4Ever," *Finalist Hysteria Anthology, 2017*; "Pinky Swear," *Foxglove Journal*; "Stepping Out," *Bending Genre*; "Eventide," *New Flash Fiction Review*

VINE LEAVES PRESS

Enjoyed this book?

Go to *vineleavespress.com* to find more.

www.ingramcontent.com/pod-product-compliance
Lightning Source LLC
LaVergne TN
LVHW061253060426
835507LV00017B/2051